THE BLACK HILLS ADVENTURE

Advanced Reader

Written and Illustrated by
Gary Harbo

May 15, 1997

Published by KUTIE KARI BOOKS, INC.

The Black Hills Adventure

Advanced Reader

ISBN 1-884149-13-8

Visit Gary's website: *www.garyharbo.com*

or write to:
Kutie Kari Books
2461 Blueberry St.
Inver Grove Hts., MN 55076
1-800-395-8843

Beauty of the Hills

The beauty of the hills, are a sight to see;
They are strong and majestic, covered in trees.

With jagged granite needles, thrust high in the sky,
Soaring out of the clouds, you can watch the eagles fly.

They hold a native people, that are much like the land;
Strong and rugged, united they stand.

Asking little from others, they honor the earth;
Unlike many cultures, nature is the key to their worth.

For every creature has a purpose, every plant has a power;
You must live the experience, or salvation will not come in the last hour.

The eagles are holy, they fly in the heavens where Wakan Tanka reins;
The buffalo is sacred, for the Lakota Sioux's life flows through their veins.

The earth has the power to heal, and the ability to grow;
There is a strength in their belief, that the proud Lakota Sioux know.

Gary Harbo

Grannie Jannie had called everybody together to announce the wonderful news. She had just purchased a huge recreational vehicle (RV) and wanted to celebrate by taking everyone on a vacation in the Black Hills of South Dakota. She had already cleared it with their parents.

"Are you serious?" Kari, Herby, Brandon and Brittany shouted in excitement. "That would be totally awesome!" they cheered as they quickly ran home to pack.

When they got back and finished loading up, it suddenly struck them that Bart and Slimey the Snake were no where to be found. That was strange. Bart seemed to be the one most excited about the trip.

"Bart!" they yelled, while frantically searching the area. Kari checked inside the RV but came up empty. Suddenly they spotted Slimey hanging over the roof.

"I've got first dibs on this spot," Bart smiled from the top. They all began to laugh. Bart looked like he was sunbathing on the beach. Grannie Jannie, however, was not amused. "Get down here!" she yelled to the two on the roof. "You're not riding up there!"

Bart began to climb down. Grannie rolled her eyes when he missed the last step and fell to the ground.

1

After loading everyone into the RV, Grannie hit the road. By the time the sun was edging into the western horizon, they were within an hour of the Black Hills. They decided to stop and spend the night in the Badlands.

As they piled out of the vehicle, Bart thought that this was the perfect time to do a little exploring on his own. Without giving Slimey a chance to object, he grabbed the snake and took off in the opposite direction of everyone else. Nobody noticed because they were captivated by the view.

"This is breathtaking!" Kari gasped as they came to the edge of the cliff. "I've never seen anything so beautiful in all my life."

"I read about this area." Herby said to the group. "The earth contains layers of pink and brown sandstone which has been washed away over the course of 37 million years. The Lakota Sioux Indians still live on this land. In fact I think they call this the Pine Ridge Indian Reservation. Wow! Look at that huge eagle soaring high over the ridges. Hey Bart, have you ever seen a bird so big in your life?"

Turning to get Bart's reaction, they discovered that he was gone. Suddenly, they heard a scream in the distance. It was Slimey the Snake and it sounded like his life was in danger. They quickly raced toward the awful sound.

Kari's heart was pounding in her throat when she saw Bart teasing a baby eagle with Slimey the Snake. She raced over and grabbed Bart's huge arm.

"Help!" Slimey screamed as he saw the baby eagles mouth open wide in anticipation. "Let me loose, Bart!!! This eagle is hungry. Look at his eyes. Help!"

"Don't worry, Slimey," Bart chuckled as the eagle lunged towards Slimey and missed. "He couldn't even get his mouth around you. You're way too big. I'm just having some fun with this little runt!"

"Bart!" Herby and Kari yelled at the top of their voices. "Quit teasing that baby eagle. You're giving Slimey a heart attack. Besides, the mother eagle looks very angry!"

"I'm just having a little fun. Nobody's going to get hurt." Bart replied. "Hey! What mother eagle? You mean this thing is just a baby! I wonder how big the parents get?" Bart asked nervously as he heard the sound of huge wings beating the air overhead.

Suddenly, out of thin air, a huge hand with the strength of steel grabbed Bart. Blackfoot was an Indian chief that watched over the land. He didn't take kindly to anyone messing around with eagles.

Blackfoot looked at Bart sternly and gave him a quick lesson on the tradition and culture of the Lakota Sioux Nation. He spoke of how the Great Spirit, *Wakan-Tanka*, is within all things: the trees, the grasses, the rivers, the mountains, the animals, the birds, and the people. The Great Spirit made all animals for a special purpose. They must be treated with respect."

"What's so special about the eagle?" Bart quietly asked.

"The Spotted Eagle, *Wanbli Gleshka*, flies highest of all created creatures and sees everything. The feathers are regarded as rays of the sun. When a feather is worn by the Indian people, it represents the presence of *Wakan-Tanka*. The eagle watches over everyone. By teasing the baby eagle, you are disrespecting the Great Spirit. You are fortunate that I came along before the mother eagle taught you a lesson of respect the hard way!" Blackfoot scolded Bart.

"Okay, okay. I'm sorry. I didn't mean any harm. I was just having a little fun with Slimey the Snake. Boy, look at the time. I hate to run, but I guess it's time we get back to the RV. I'm sorry Mrs. Eagle," Bart mumbled as he hustled out of her way.

The next morning Grannie Jannie woke everybody up early. She wanted to get into the Black Hills as soon as possible. After Bart's encounter with the angry eagle, he was quite subdued and eager to leave the area. The last thing he wanted to see was that huge eagle again.

Kari noticed Bart's sullen mood so she decided to cheer him up. "Hey, Grannie," Kari said, "Let's go to Mt. Rushmore first! Let's show Bart the awesome carvings of Washington, Jefferson, Roosevelt and Lincoln." When Grannie agreed, they all began to get packed up.

Once they arrived at the site, Bart wanted his picture taken in front of the huge monument. Kari, Herby, and Slimey gathered around while Grannie Jannie took the picture.

After they had their pictures taken, Grannie explained how Mt. Rushmore was carved out of the hard granite stone by Gutzon Borglum. In 1927 he was commissioned to build this tremendous tribute to the great leaders of our country. It took 7 years of carving spread out over a 14 year time-span and over 400 workers to finish this great wonder. The crew removed over 500,000 tons of stone before it was finally completed on October 31, 1941. Gutzon had died that spring, so his son Lincoln had to finish the task.

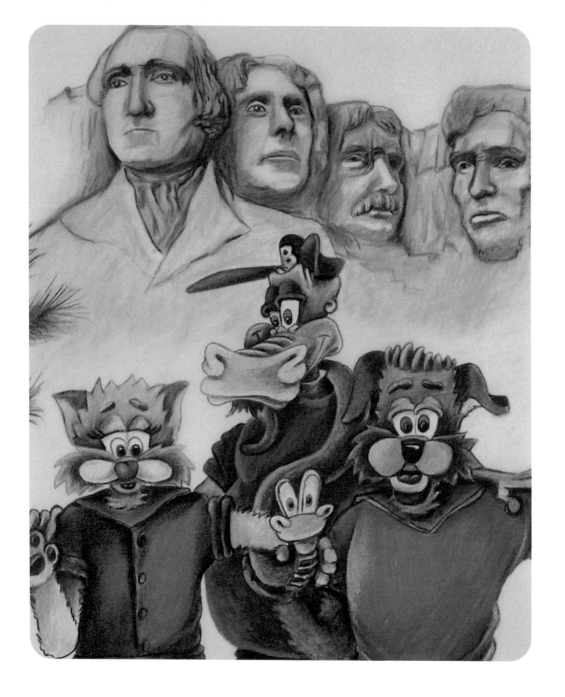

11

After exploring the trails around Mt. Rushmore, they jumped into the RV, drove around the corner, and discovered Horse Thief Lake. That's were they decided to camp.

Before Grannie could even get supper started, Bart was racing over to check out the steep granite cliffs. Huffing and puffing, he struggled to reach the top. Once he made it, he was surprised to see Brandon, Brittany, and Slimey the Snake swimming in the water below. Realizing that he smelled like an old bear from the climb, he dove off the cliff and hollered, "Yee-hah. Look out below!"

Brandon and Brittany saw the accident waiting to happen and dove for the bottom of the lake. Slimey, however wasn't so lucky. Since he was wrapped around the inner tube, he couldn't react in time. He was still lying on the tube when Bart's head streaked right through the middle. The impact sent Slimey flying high into the air. Bart and the tube went crashing under water. Brandon and Brittany were nearly washed ashore by the monstrous wave. As Slimey landed in another part of the lake, Bart came up gasping for air. His arms, pinned to his side, were wedged tightly in the tube. "Help, help!!" Bart screamed in fear. Acting quickly, Kari, Herby, Brandon, and Brittany hauled him ashore and spent the better part of an hour pulling the tube off. Bart was still a little shaken as they headed back to camp for supper.

After a good nights sleep, Bart was ready for action. "Let's go explore the needles!" Bart yelled as they finished Grannie Jannie's awesome breakfast.

"Go ahead," Grannie said, "I'll clean up the RV and figure out how we can get to Lake Pactola."

Bart and the gang took off hiking towards the tall pillars of granite rock. The pillars were called needles because the tall narrow peaks almost looked like a series of huge needles pointing towards the sky.

They began to climb the narrow winding trail leading up the needles. "Hey! Wait for me everybody!" Bart yelled gasping for air. "I can't keep up because I have to carry this oversized snake."

"Right, Bart," Kari laughed, "I'm sure it doesn't have anything to do with that spare tire you're carrying."

"Hey, I'm just a growing boy!" Bart wheezed as he removed Slimey from his neck. "You're on your own, snake!" Bart growled after Slimey told him that the only growing he did was horizontal.

After spending the morning at the needles, they all headed back to camp to help Grannie get the RV ready for travel.

14

15

The whole gang was mind boggled as they drove over the dam on Lake Pactola. Brandon and Brittany decided to go swimming. Herby and Kari wanted to try the fishing. instead. Bart had never fished before, but the thought of catching a big one definitely had his interest.

While Brandon and Brittany changed into their suits, Kari and Herby rented a boat. Bart, Slimey and Herby barely had their feet in the boat, before Kari started the motor and took off to find a fishing spot.

Bart learned how to cast and was soon showing off. He swung his arm in a wide arc and let the line go zipping out far into the lake. When it hit the water, a huge bass jumped out of the water, grabbed the bait, and took off in a splash.

"I got one!" Bart screamed as the pole bent in half. Bart yanked the rod and reeled it in with all of his might. It almost looked like the fish was water skiing as Bart yanked it towards the boat. Bart was so excited he didn't even hear Kari when she hollered for him to stop squashing her. Slimey got the fish lips in his face when the bass was pulled into the boat. As Bart stood up to celebrate, he lost his balance and fell overboard with a tremendous splash. Bart shot to the surface and wanted to know what had happened to his fish. Luckily, Herby had a good grip on the line and was able to hold onto the "great catch".

16

After pulling Bart back into the boat, they hurried back to the shore to tell Brittany and Brandon about Bart's first fish. Bart was wet and tired, but proud as a peacock. Grannie couldn't believe her ears. She laughed as she cooked a delicious meal of fresh fish.

The next morning Grannie dropped them all off at a horse ranch nestled on a flat meadow under Harney Peak. Bart was bummed out when he heard that they couldn't find a horse big enough for him. Of the dozens of horses, there wasn't a single one that was willing to try lifting his massive weight.

"Go ahead," Bart moaned as they began to ride the trails, "I'll hike some of the trails. Don't worry about me!" Bart whined, hoping that they'd feel sorry for him and not go on the ride.

"Okay, Bart!" Kari, Brandon, Herby, Slimey, and Brittany shouted as they rode off down the trail.

Bart hung his head and began to walk along another trail. Little did he know that Custer State Park had over 1,500 buffalo roaming the range. After walking a few miles, he began to see these massive animals on the horizon. He could hardly believe his luck. With his heart pounding at his chest he closed in on these huge animals.

17

18

Meanwhile, back on the other trail were five of the happiest creatures on earth. Herby and Kari were in the lead when their horses carried them to a clearing on the trail. That's when they discovered Sylvan Lake. When Brandon, Brittany and Slimey the Snake came to the opening, they were truly stunned by the beauty. It was times like this that made them reflect on how lucky they were to be alive. These Black Hills were simply one breathtaking view after another.

"Wow..." Herby sighed, "It's too bad Bart and Grannie couldn't be here to share in the moment. This is something I'll never forget. It's so peaceful."

"Well then, it's probably good that Bart's not here," Slimey the Snake chuckled, "otherwise it certainly wouldn't be peaceful."

"I wonder what Bart is up to," Brandon asked as everyone got off their horses to enjoy a picnic lunch.

"He's probably back at the RV eating Grannie out of house and home!" Brittany chuckled as she passed out the sandwiches and drinks. "Make sure you pack up your garbage so we can leave this spot they same way we found it!" she said as the lunch quickly disappeared.

Little did they know how much trouble Bart was about to get himself into. After Bart found this herd of huge buffalo, he climbed high onto the rocks above where the largest buffalo was grazing. Bart leaped from the top of the rocks and landed smack on top of the buffalo's back. Within the skip of a heart beat, Bart had the bull by the horn and was in for the ride of his life.

"Yee-ha!" Bart roared with delight as he stuck his feet high in the air. "Come on grandpa, let's see what you got!"

Now the buffalo was by no means amused. In fact, he was ready to explode. Not only had Bart nearly given him a heart attack with the surprise jump, but the weight of this oversized ton of bricks landing on his back nearly broke him in two. The buffalo lowered his head and tore off across the meadow like his tail was on fire.

The way this animal was snorting and charging, Bart realized that the situation was totally out of control. "Whoa, boy! Whoa!!!!" Bart began to scream at the top of his voice. "Help! Help! Someone get me off this demon. Help me!"

Herby, Kari and the rest of the group heard Bart's yells far off in the distance and quickly made their way to a clearing by the cliff. It sounded like a life and death matter, and they soon found out that it was all of that and more.

22

23

They broke through the clearing just in time to see the heart-stopping scene unfold. Bart was racing towards the edge of a cliff on the back of a stampeding buffalo. Just when it seemed that they were both going to race right over the edge, the buffalo lowered his head and launched Bart like a rocket. Bart tumbled head over heels screaming for help. His eyes were big as saucers as he flapped his arms frantically in the air. His heart pounded in his chest as he fell head first toward the canyon.

"Bart! Grab the bush!" Kari and Herby screamed.

Hearing the yells of his friends, Bart frantically clawed his arms towards the bush. He was able to grab hold of a branch that was well rooted into a small enclave on the side of the cliff. Hanging on for dear life, his body crashed to the wall as the branch bent in half. Luckily, it held. He quickly dug his toes deep into the canyon cracks to get his weight off the tree that was beginning to give way. Bart was terrified, but was safe for as long as he could hold onto the wall.

"Please help me!!!" Bart pleaded to his friends. "Hurry up. I don't know how long I can hang on. Please hurry!"

Kari, Brittany, Herby and Brandon didn't need any encouragement from Bart. They knew he was in a dangerous situation and were already streaking towards the horses.

Brittany was leading the pack as they began the race against time across Custer State Park. As they tore around the rim of the canyon, Brittany's horse had to leap high over the rocks on the path. As her horse came crashing down, she found herself sailing out of the saddle. Grabbing the saddle horn in mid air she hung on for dear life.

"Whoa!" Brittany yelled as she was flapping in the wind.

At that precise moment, Brandon's horse had found the rocks and was in the middle of its high leap. Brandon was jarred so far back that he could see the ground behind him. In fact, the horses tail came up and swished him across his eyes as they landed. As Brandon was jolted back up into his saddle he saw that Brittany had pulled herself back up.

Kari was on a mission as she leaned her body into the sprinting mare. This ride was becoming dangerous, but she just didn't care. Bart was in trouble and nothing was going to slow her down.

As they approached the spot where Bart had been thrown over the rocks, they heard him yelling for help. They also saw the eagle that Bart had tangled with in the Badlands. This was not a good time for the big bird to be looking for revenge. Bart was in major trouble. This Black Hills adventure was quickly turning into the Black Hills disaster.

25

Bart trembled in his britches as he spotted the eagle in the distance. He'd been holding onto the cliff for so long that his arms felt like pieces of rubber. His muscles were so tired that his legs and arms were shaking uncontrollably. Just as he was about to give up, he heard the sound of his friends' voices.

"Hang on, Bart!" Kari, Herby, Brittany and Brandon yelled as they came to the edge. "We'll save you buddy!"

Herby had the best idea. They could throw him a rope and pull him up to safety. After Slimey pointed out that they didn't have any rope, Kari looked long and hard at Slimey.

"Oh no, you're not using me!" Slimey quickly said. "NO WAY! That big moose would pull me in half. He weighs too much. Just forget it! You'll have to think of something else."

"Come on, Slimey." Kari begged. "We have to try. He's your best friend, and he needs you now more than ever."

"All right" Slimey sighed as they threw him over the cliff. Bart almost cried when he saw his friends helping him out. He grabbed a hold of Slimey's neck like hot gum sticks to a shoe. They pulled with every ounce of energy, but Bart didn't budge. Slimey was nearly choked to death before they realized that it wasn't going to work. As Bart let go of Slimey's neck, he saw the eagle swooping down to finish him off.

28

"Oh noooo!" Bart screamed as the eagles powerful talons grabbed him by the pants. Bart was so frightened that he nearly passed out. This eagle was big enough to actually lift him off the rocks. He quickly closed his eyes. He could hear the swishing of the giant wings as the mother eagle strained to create air flow. He could feel the strain of her body as she attempted to back away from the cliff. Then he lost his stomach as they dropped in a free fall. She fought desperately for enough wind to support her tremendous load.

It was then that Bart and his friends realized that this eagle was risking her life to rescue him. If this was just an act of revenge, then the eagle would have dropped him by now. She was determined to help this crazy city slicker get out of trouble.

As they accelerated down the canyon, the eagle finally achieved enough velocity to create the necessary lift to begin a gradual climb to safety. As they flew to safety in front of Crazy Horse Mountain, Bart was thanking Wakan-Tanka for the magnificent eagle guarding it's heavens.

"Look", Brittany laughed, as she pointed in the air. "Bart's flying by the seat of his pants!"

Brandon and Herby were nearly rolling on the ground at the sight. Kari was laughing so hard her sides began to hurt.

31

As they were enjoying their sidesplitting laugh, the eagle lightly set Bart down and returned high into the sky.

Herby, Kari, Brittany and Brandon raced over to Bart and gave him a hand up. He was never so glad to see them in his whole entire life. In fact, he did a lot of soul searching as they returned to the RV.

Grannie couldn't believe what had happened to him. "What a way to end our vacation," she said as they packed up the RV for the return trip home. "The trip back always goes really fast. In fact, it'll fly right by!" she laughed at Bart.

As they drove out of the Black Hills and headed home through the Bad Lands, Bart laid his head on the RV's console and sighed, "I'm sorry I messed up this vacation."

Kari put her arms around Bart and gave him a big hug. Herby grabbed him by the arm and told him he was first class. Brandon and Brittany said that he was the life of the party.

Slimey was getting sick of it all. "Sure, I stick my neck out to help you, but you get all the compliments. All I got was an extra foot added to my body length." Slimey moaned.

As they all laughed, Grannie told Bart that he was welcome on any trip. It wouldn't be the same without him.

THE END

Gary Harbo grew up in Lynd, a small rural community in Southwestern, Minnesota. He founded KUTIE KARI BOOKS, Inc. in 1990 and now lives in the St. Paul area. Gary's books and cartoon characters were inspired by his love and appreciation for his children, Kari (14) and Gary II (13).

As an author and illustrator, Gary teaches art lessons to over 25,000 elementary school children every year. His motivational talks encompass the whole process of writing, illustrating and publishing. His talks include; Keynote speaker for the International Reading Association, Chapter One Parent/Children Workshops, guest author for Southwest and Northeast Minnesota Young Authors Conferences, Rotary Club motivational talks, as well as Author-in-Residence for hundreds of schools in seven different states.

His love of drawing began at an early age and has resulted in several first place finishes in art competitions for his colored pencil illustrations. His work is mostly in wildlife and cartooning.

Gary graduated with high honors from South Dakota School of Mines and Technology (SDSM&T) in 1983 with a B.S. in Electrical Engineering. During his senior year at SDSM&T, Gary's interest in children spawned his original design of a Crib Death Detector. He created this invention for his newborn daughter, Kari. It won him national acclaim with a 2nd place finish in the Institute of Electrical and Electronic Engineering finals in Houston, Texas.

In 1983 Gary accepted a management position at US West Communications and spent 8 years developing marketing systems in Aberdeen, SD., Omaha, NE., Phoenix, AZ and Minneapolis, MN. His creative design of the first-of-its-kind Market Intelligence System culminated in his reception of a US West Communications Presidential award in 1991.

In March of 1991, Gary resigned from his analytical career to pursue his lifelong dream of working with children. His Minnesota based company, KUTIE KARI BOOKS Inc., has published five exciting picture books, **My New Friend**, **Bad Bart's Revenge**, **Bart Becomes a Friend**, **The Great Train Ride** and **The Black Hills Adventure**. These action-packed adventures are bringing smiles to tens of thousands of children across the Midwest.

For more information on ordering books or receiving information on school visits, write or call:

KUTIE KARI BOOKS, Inc.
2461 Blueberry St.
Inver Grove Heights, MN 55076
612-450-7427 or 1-800-395-8843

Bart and His Circle of Friends